POETIC REALMS

POETIC REALMS

INCLUDING WESTON-SUPER-MARE SEASHORE TRAIL

By

ANTHONY KEYES

First published in 1999

Published by:
Atlantique

U.K.
British Library Cataloguing in Publication Data: A CIP record for this book is available from the British Library.

Front cover: An original Icelandic photograph by Anthony Keyes

Printed by:
ProPrint
Riverside Cottage
Great North Road
Stibbington
Peterborough PE8 6LR

ISBN: 0 9533809 0 4

CONTENTS: PAGE NO:

PAGE NO

+ These poems are from the Weston-super-Mare Seashore Trail

FOREWORD

For several years past I have seen and commended Anthony Keyes' poems in the North Somerset Poetry Competition, and it is a particular pleasure to be asked to write this foreword to his new book 'POETIC REALMS.'

As a writer of books that are 'different' I enjoyed his unique insight, and the blend of poems and pictures on a wide range of subjects. The style suits the subject, and many of the pictures are quite early and rare photographs.

Landscapes, seascapes, people, places rural and urban, the West Country, the North Country and Iceland all have mention, and the pictures range from humorous to solemn.

A tribute to Diana, Princess of Wales, and an illustrated memorial to the ship 'TITANIC' are also here, together with First World War Soldiers and Weston Holidaymakers in both words and pictures, plus Sir Stanley Matthews as bonus.

In a push-button era of ephemeral messages, it is good to find someone who is expressing permanent concerns in a way to command long-term interest.

For all these reasons I am pleased to commend this book of Anthony Keyes' poetry, and hope for more books to follow.

Bill Pickard

BILL PICKARD

Bill Pickard has judged many major poetry competitions, including the famous Cheltenham Festival of Literature

INTRODUCTION

Poetic Realms is a Unique collection of poetic dimensions.

Each poem is very different from the next. Travelling through the pages of Poetic Realms is a journey through time; a visit to many different areas.

In some cases there are never before published illustrations which convey the feelings of the individual poems.

Poetic Realms is an appreciation of profound psychological insights to savour and real life social observations. Feel the music of life, place yourself within the poems.

A book with a difference, Poetic Realms is full of variety and introduces for the first time the new and exciting panoramic Weston-super-Mare Seashore Trail.

When visiting the poetry trail you can discover the spirit of the poem for yourself. A map is included at the back of this book giving details of the locations and settings for the poems.

Poetic Realms is a book to relish, the perfect companion a fascinating experience.

GUARDIAN ANGEL

Contact
Hold on tight for this flight.
We leave the air strip of green with soaring hearts.
An upward lift, skyward bound, far from the ground.
The wooden propeller speeding, round.

Skyride mist, the elixir of life, cutting through the frosty ice,
Passing the speeding aeronautics of torn billowing clouds.
Lunging into the vigorous nothingness abyss.
A wing and a prayer for those who dare.
'I will never leave thee, nor forsake thee.' Hebrews.ch.13.5.

The wonderful world of the elevated aviator.
Whisking whirlwind skyholes with double barrel heart rolls.
Swooping to looping loops.
Secured by a shadow and a strong seat belt.
No cockpit canopy for me, no parachute, what a hoot.

Thrown back into the seat by the shout of the wind.
Cold savage skies, wide opening eyes,
Enhancing and magnifying, all around vision.
With twin circle goggles the mind begins to boggle.
Solid and unyielding, the heavy flying jacket.

Shattering the silence, an airspace crescendo
Oscillating the vertical speed indicator.
Pulsing throttle roars of the screaming engine
Muffled by the soft leather flying helmet,
Flowing is the silken white trailing scarf.

Life is full of leaps and bounds
Ups and downs, spin rolls and side slip dips.
When you land upon the ground,
Even if you tumble and fall,
The Lord will be with you through it all.

WISDOM FOR CHANGE

As I look up into the wider sky,
I look around and wonder why.
Lock, stock and barrel, before us.
A new year's carol.

The man in the sky looks down from upon high.
Sudden second thoughts, arrival of the sky sorting station.
Join hands now across the nation.
Hear the acoustic shouts from the dawning of antiquity
To playful plate tectonics.

What on earth are we doing?
2000 twelve month environmental revolutions.
Here is planet earth's green new year's resolution.
For in Somerset we have reasons.
Our wish to keep the seasons.
Ticking restful yearling hours, strike forth.

Pointing are millennium midnight hands
From the Weston town hall, stone clock tower.
Captive above, the global barren moon's retrospective gaze.
Strumming my song to strolling feet.
Lyrical emotional rhythms of pounding heartbeats.
From the birth of a child to the grandfather of time.
Twenty centurian years, each day, a new year's day!

A Happy New Year

CHARLOTTE

As the waters cover the sea
I shall wait as land to meet thee,
For tomorrow has no time to borrow
Loving memories live as treasure.

Once a time honoured cobble street, now concrete.
Fond reminisces of old Bristol suburbs
With iron edge kerbs.
Four Vine Row, seems so long ago.

A fine lady my Great-Grandmother O'Connell,
Born 1864. Oh to have knocked at her door.
For her kindness and welcome glow
She was known so well.

Only fragments of imagination remain,
If I could pull up a pew
In her cottage
I never knew.

Charlotte O'Connell
1864 - 1931

THE TIDAL TRAIL

I thought I saw you there
In the sunshine of Weston-super-Mare
Following the poetry tidal trail.
Walking to marvellous places, viewing seasonal graces.
North Somerset's jubilant, serene seafront.
The strolling peaceful promenade romances
With happy sea song acknowledging glances.
A sun dance glare, Royal Parades fine air.

I thought I saw your golden light
In the breaking waves of the Tropicana night.
The rhythms of the sea bring it all home to me.
From Uphill's adventure to Middle Hope Cove I venture
The natural harmony, the spring, the fall
Weston's poetic seaside trail has it all.

Refer to the Tropicana on 'The Seashore Trail' Map Page 62

WE ARE ENJOYING OURSELVES
A.1.
AT WESTON-SUPER-MARE

MIDNIGHT MUSIC

Rock pool footprints unfold like the accordion
Mesmerising high cirrus clouds until the returning current.
Rhapsody wind crescendo shiver the senses
As they perform a seaspray melody
Lyrically the night chills to cold.

Slippery seaweed hugs part submerged boulders
Protecting from the driver's drift overture
Wave compositions serenade Middle Hope Cove
As the full blooded sun drowns to silence.
A lullaby sunset flashes colours to their sleep.

Grey moon pebbles, roll as sea shanty songs
While waning disco lights ripen to blackness.
The blustery midnight blue notes wash away recollection.
Nocturnally muddy salt tides hide your reflection.
Grass like violin strings cut through the hearts logic.

Dark green walks waltz upon purple thistles.
Sloping lyceum sea fields, revealed their epistles
To a minstrel symphony,
Of dreams and desires
For our hearts to aspire.

Refer to Middle Hope Cove on 'The Seashore Trail' Map
Page 62

STORM TEARS

Hands grasp the reins,
Flowing water gains.
Glistening illuminated,
Electric ice raindrops on glass.
Pitter-patter, wet shiny coated matter.
The light glows dim.
Interstella blinking,
Thinking washed away for another day.
Beacons hidden in translucent heaven,
Descending from the Constellation,
The starlight is real.
The frame of the window sealed with a vision.
Double glazed disguised in the haze.
Smiling, beguiling,
Semi-detached, the gate on the latch.
A misty face conjures thoughts of theosophy,
And a friend from the nostalgic era.
Cracking thunder, spiting lights of fire.
Empty cloud bursts leave feelings of hope.
A new day conceived,
The transcendental curtain unfolds,
For all of this has been foretold.

THE FESTIVAL

Hearing with straining eyes,
The sharp knock of the willow, audible in crisp air.
Sight-screens, the far of the green.
Seated umpires, watch the ricocheting bright young things,
Giving counsel to one another.
All against one.

The lone defender, fights to survive
Those intent on bowling him into oblivion,
Back to the pavilion.
One slip and he's stumped,
Left to look a chump.

Turning heads observe the imminent interval.
The rumbling tumbling rattling trolley wheels,
Scorch the tarmac path, with the two large
Metal teapots steaming past,
Onto the padded warlords.
A rasping tractor kick starts into life.
Watching experts confer with a friend called drink.
If I was out there....

A new beginning, a new over.
Time runs out.
The sleeping Texan with the white stetson
Never moved from his seat,
At least he was there in spirit.
The things those people said,
Most unfair.
After all, it's just not cricket.
Or is it not just festivity.

RECONCILIATION

The Spinning coin of the realm, the King at the helm.
Our tomorrow's restored, we recall the drum,
A distant beat of marching feet.
Fifty years ago; it became so.
Bravery not slavery, the price they paid.
Happy Isles, the sorry state.

Battle cries, closing out the skies.
Barrage and bombardment.
Birds of prey, fighting view, by the few.
Sons and daughters to overcome the slaughter.
One more new life in all that strife,
The cry of salvation, a baby, maybe.

Liberty remembers our defenders,
No quarter asked for, no quarter given.
Plane targets, concealed in the shield,
Machines they said, not men.
Smoking gatling gunnery, sights the sacrifice,
Freedom is peace.

Safeguarded, homeguarded,
Dissolution of protracted science,
No reliance upon compliance,
No absolution to the final solution,
Tribal trickery, trespassing the truth.
Recorded black and white vision, on the television.

Dust from the war cloud settles, the monarch reigns,
Rejoice in green sunlit uplands,
No more sinister birds from the eagle's nest.
Heaven safe keep awake,
Do not forget our Soldiers wake,
Enlist with peace, let all hostilities cease.

SEASCAPE

Oh compass needle point to me
This fair town upon the Severn sea.
Her horizon moored alongside the
Radiance of golden sands below.
With inshore winds a blow,
Behold her welcome smile aglow.
Twinkling diamonds of twilight sun
Settle upon blue yonder seas.
Ship and shore, so much to explore.
Quarrelsome waters mingle with
Rabble-rousing Weston rock.
Plenty of dunes with glades.
Just right for buckets and spades.
Sea-salt water a rush, grinding pebbles
To sand dust.
Castle flags once proud, now left to collect,
No more to protect.
Raging leaping waves, the surf arrives,
Helped along with sunshine, rain and song.
The compass arrow, in blue sea mist,
The pier, points to triumphal twirling
Deep water secret thoughts, beneath the
Sounds of rolling bygone breakers.
Showerproof views of Holmes from afar.
One steep, one flat,
With roofs of sky and stars.
Under mystical mosaic clouds,
We laugh, and cry.
For we came to rest our hearts
Beneath a Weston sky.

Refer to Grand Pier on 'The Seashore Trail' Map Page 62.

The Grand Pier, Weston-super-Mare.
First day opening queues in 1904.

ORCHESTRA OF LIGHT

Late in the morn is the Icelandic dawn.
Bright, white light.
Horizontal golden gilt-edged rays
Warming the coldness of days.
Extreme dreams of snowfall abound,
Little time for play, the shortness of each day.

From the smouldering steam mist soup of creation
Have risen iceberg volcanoes.
Barren are the unexplored lava lands
Fear not, bathe in the warmth of nature's lagoons.
Outside is the edge, the frosts, bites.
Remember not to get lost to the frost.

For faint hearts,
Rise the evaporated rainbow paths.
Pointing above majestic walls of crashing waterfalls.
All too soon comes the creeping night of moon
Consuming mountains and high river gushing fountains
With a strange charm that explores God's Kingdom.

As the light fades, stars shine brighter
Making the land lighter.
Sulphur black volcanic sand disappears,
The snow nowhere to go, reflects upwards
Into a midnight moon sky
Awaiting God's welcome, a new dawning.

A wilderness, a land for all seasons,
The reason for the rainbow,
To link heaven and earth,
To see God,
In a new light

HAWORTH HEARTS

Behold this parsonage,
I call my heart.
Warmth from within,
Without a lonely sweeping moor,
A remote wilderness.
The mare lost upon a desolate
Mossy moor.
Thy stallion away from the battalion.

Heavens frozen teardrops,
Bouncing on a cold flagstone face.
Life, but a moment in time,
'Tis thy seconds, that make these years.
They say the garden
Had never looked so good,
Methinks, I have seen the wet winter shades,
The strife, rainfall brought forth new life.

Hath not bulb tips been pressing
With mirth for hours,
Fighting to become flowers.
Mischievous, the chorus,
Oh lark sing for me the song of thy poem.
Right for the taking, left a heart aching.
No curtain in the glittering looking-glass
Window can hide the echoes of footsteps past.

Meteorological memoirs chiselled,
By thy stone hearth.
'Tis no more warmed by the fanning flame.
Outside the spirit of the grave yard.
A meeting place for life and death.
Hark! the incumbent church tower holds counsel,
To opinion of the angry anguished, invisible,
Unremitting wind.

Gargoyles gaze upon
Yellowed stone moss,
Irksome heather and bramble,
Amongst the weathered
Tapered walk.
If thou kiss given, as if a gilt-edge brow
Of the rolling dales
Freedom be mine.

'Twas silver sunlit branches
Ripped from thee,
Torn apart, as dust in wind
Cracking twigs underfoot
Carried whence its source
To a flowing stream
No one,
Mused the scream.

Love as if eternity
It came,
As if from eternity
So doth it go.
As water vapour rays
Scattered in the morn moor haze.
Reflective eyes
As the Golden Eagle sighs.

Its shadow cutting across the spirit
Of the moor-lapped grey stone home,
Solitude pools of water,
Mere mirrors, prisoners of light.
My soul hears distance tones
Of messenger Bells and church tower hours.
For thou self time with fate
Will not wait, nor hesitate.

CRYSTAL CLEAR

There may be a small flickering light
In the grate, such is fate.
There may be straw on the floor,
Such is the luck of the draw.

Thatched yola warmth within,
Not tainted by sin.
A brass door handle,
Another welcome angle.

Palaces with cold celebrant treasures.
Happy are the precious hidden troves.
Remember the brilliance of a warm welcome.
Leading lights of moments, make the meaning.

'Tis friendship and joy, beautified
With captured purity, an encouraging word.
Life springs forward from the non materialistic
Humble garden.

Cultivate hope in abundance.
Beware transparent silicon stardust smiles,
The bizarre ice camo stares.
Two up, two down, never a frown.

Seize the life of thy spiritual
Sands of time, rich vital gems,
Never repeated always treasured,
Shining forth with crystal sparkles of wisdom.

LEGACY

Anticipation before every game.
The waiting, the build up.
Screeched notes of the steel whistle
Rebounding against the crowd's roar.
Awaiting the score.
Destiny, a legend to be fulfilled.

Now retired, only because it was required.
'I wish I was out there playing.'
Laments the maestro, as the wing commander's
Famous feet begin to edge toward the
Touch line.
Thoughts of heading every ball, meeting every cross.

There will always be a man called Sir Stan.
On every pitch with blades of grass
His name will always be said.
Playing for future generations.
A wizard of a hero.
Whom seldom saw zero..

Sir Stanley Matthews.
More time, than a second for every fan.
A hat-trick of a man, the young inspired.
Their fathers' knowingly admire.
Stan is one of their fold.
That's how this poem is told.

Sir Stanley Matthews
at Clevedon Town Football Club
30th July 1995.
Photo by Bristol Evening Post.

STARLIGHT

Why are you so frightened?
How is it that you have no faith? Mark: 4:40
Pure pelting melting snowflakes blur our winter vision.
Taste is their disappearance, a strange calm, no alarm.
Snow on the Weston shore, crunching slush, ice melt waters rush.

Energised bouncing water diamond lights fall sparkling in darkness
Purity is positive, an energy source, a new life cause.
When our bodies are bereft of their purpose.
We will arrive safe, our spirits lift, is God's gift,
To a place without time, a welcome glow and friends you know.

Burying your head in the sand, leaves grit in your eyes.
Bright are the colours of light with all thy holy might.
The one true God, no time to plod.
No deja blue, you will rise, starlight in your eyes.
Words and vision breathe new life, far away the fading strife.

Happy are the dissolving murmuring sand ripples that dance
At the spiritual water's edge as they are consumed
By the moon's tidal wave. so shall we change
With the feel of the flowing holy spirit of God's love.
Safe as if a child's hand held in its parent's grasp.

High Tide at Weston-super-Mare.

Ellen Byrne 1858-1920

PARK STREET 1920

Life's disguise, the rush of time,
A combination of events.
Predestination of that Thursday night's lament.
At that same place today,
There is now a crossing
To help you on your way.

Oh to leave a prophecy for thee,
A remote view to the past,
To stop a present misadventure,
A motor car driver's censure.
Heavy fell the Bristol rain,
Windscreen wipers, yet to be invented.

A Ford coupe motor car was soon to be dented.
Top Speed approaching at 20 mph,
Dim of side lights, no beam of light,
No sound of horn,
Darkness all around.
Skiddy wet roadward bound.

September 30, Ellen Byrne
Went out of her front door,
At number four, their family home.
A fruit and greengrocery shop
For five years or more.
Across the road and back.

No time at all to that.
Ellen's brown coat
Did disguise her small size,
Leaving Avery's shop.
Her purchase made,
She waited outside to stop.

Ellen's journey age 62 went unseen
As she was looking towards College Green.
She saw the motor car, jerk and spurt.
A sudden change down of gear,
The lady driver did not see her.
The car leaped forth.

People saw the fall.
Ellen had no time at all.
Not even for a warning call.
The coupe slued off line
To hit that Great Grandmother of mine.
7.38 pm, Ellen arrived at heaven's gate.

Where Herbert, her son killed
In the Great war did wait.
She breathes no more
On her way back to her front door,
Where Nora, her daughter did shout
To Fenton her father who came running out.

With thanks, the ambulance service arrived,
But kind, dear Ellen
Did not survive.
Their family shop was later sold, and after change of use,
The rhyme and reason of many seasons the years did pass.
The building blew up, with a huge gas blast.

SONNET 59-15

As if from an explosion crater, the start.
To arrive, the art; a sub sixty-minute dart.
A ten-mile Wyvern run, a distance starter's gun.
Athletic saga sway, each to race their way.
Thundering arrow sure valour, pouting vest crests.
A lava tide rush, every runner avoids the crush.

Crusading miles timed to perfection, no time for correction.
Unfolding power, the glory, the pathfinder's story.
No room for doubt, fast pace throughout.
Volcanic shouts, the public address system, announce.
A welcoming call, 'Still under the hour.'
Forty-five seconds to spare, spectators cheer and stare.
A solidified moment, a personal best.
The art deco vacuum the test.

A MIRROR FOR THE CLOUDS

In the quiet
Of the evening
The rhythms
Of my breathing
Duet to the song
Of the shore.

At Glentworth Bay
A Marine Lake
Weston's mirror for the clouds.
The salt oxygen breeze
Fills my lungs with ease.
Golden sunshine holidays
The crowning grace
A jewel encased.

Refer to Marine Lake on 'The Seashore Trail' Map PAGE 62

Weston-super-Mare.

LIQUID DREAMS

Acid reindeer, why not natural rain dear,
Did you ever see nature going wrong,
I did.
Things you've heard of, wouldn't believe,
Do not try to leave or deceive.
Greed by man, no longer free by man,
Wild beasts have their feast.
Unnatural nature becomes a breaker,
Shouting you are the best,
What about the rest.
Look at your pride, why do you hide.
Unknown territory, please take no more,
Our vanishing, wild promised land.
Scars show your disgrace,
Just look at this place.
Smouldering embers,
Remembering the cold light of the harsh day.
Pulse thundering,
Striking incandescent lighting,
An oasis storm,
Soft and warm.
A second of a moment frozen.

GLACIER GARDEN

Oh! Happy Greenland, why are you so blue,
When my heart is true to be with you?
I pray and lull to temporary sleep
Your soul and mine to keep.
We float amongst the spell of natural beauty,
Your atmospheric song, a lullaby of the flautist winds.

My life, I give to you; my gain,
The prize reflected in my mystic eyes,
Your wondrous eternal smile to change my all.
Enveloping silence mists, cover your pale complexion.
Your firelight eyes melt as waters ice.
Parting with soothing teardrops, you fade to disappear.
Reach and stretch your hands to mine,
So that we may walk, together through time.

A SHOUT IN THE DARK

Southampton April 10th, at high noon tide.
It's 1912, It's unsinkable, It's unthinkable.
175 feet high, with four huge funnels.
First, second, third class, a ship built to last.
Super luxury and gracious attention.
Many hopes, far too few life boats.
Passing sighs, crowds wave their goodbyes.

Pleasure, relaxation, a maiden Atlantic voyage,
She steamed on, into the quiet starlit night.
14th April 11.40pm, her testimony the bitterly cold calm sea.
Iceberg warning calls.
Below the water, a curious motion,
On the starboard deck passengers collect, berg souvenirs.
The ship halted.

15th April 12.45am, the wireless, the first call.
'We are the 'Titanic' sinking,
Please have your life boats ready.'
Constant rocket waves into a clear night sky,
Only the 'Carpathia' steamed to save. 705.
The fabulous Atlantic liner began to slide
A pulling ocean her guide.

Women and children lowered in boats.
Behind, an ear splitting roar of steam
The ship quaked, the funnels churned.
2.18am the lights no longer burned.
2.20am 1500 souls, the playing band;
The gallant Captain Smith's last stand.
Unpredictability is never far from sure.

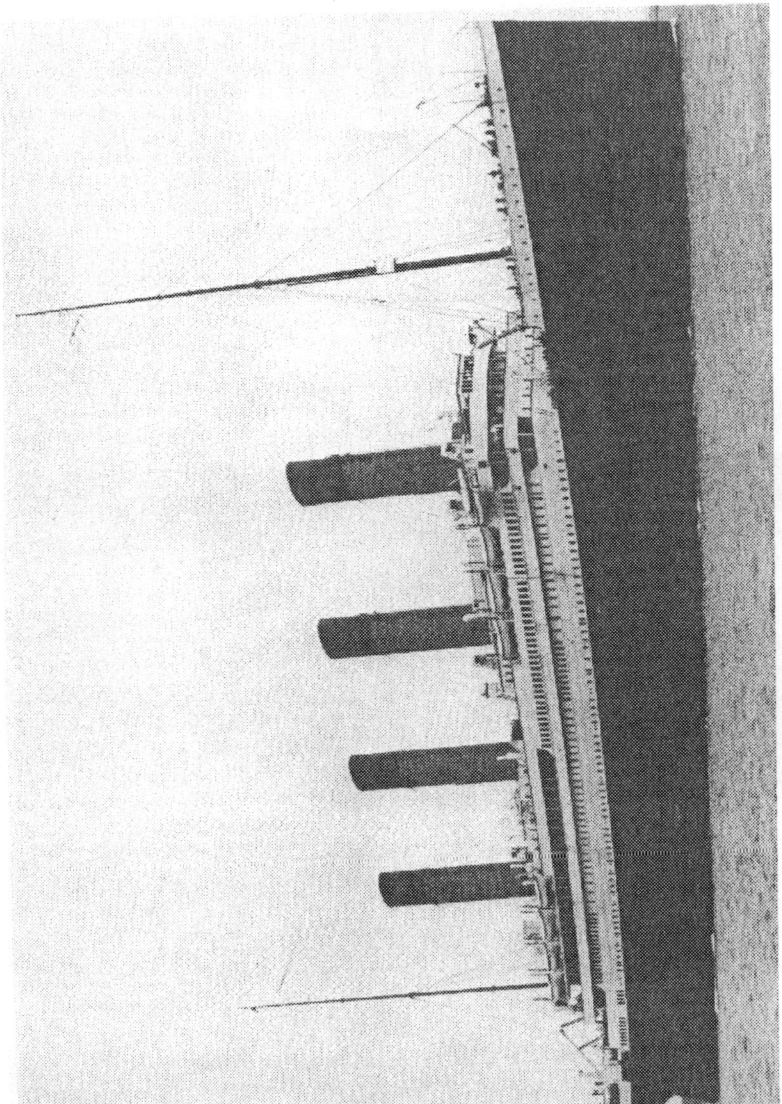

R.M.S. Titanic

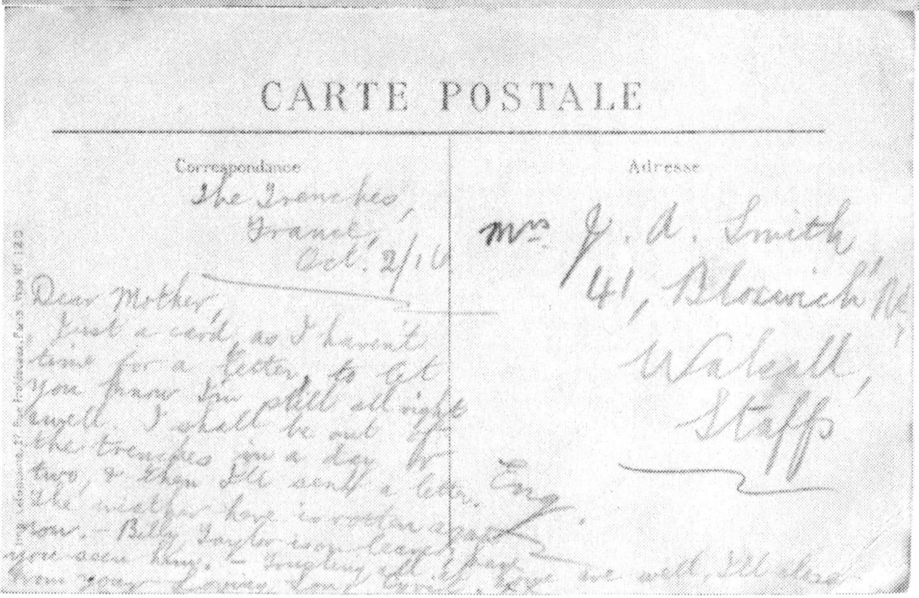

CARTE POSTALE

Correspondance

The Trenches,
France,
Oct. 2/16

Dear Mother,
Just a card as I haven't time for a letter, to let you know I'm still all right & well. I shall be out of the trenches in a day or two, & then I'll send a letter. The weather here is rather [illegible] now. — Billy Taylor is on leave [illegible] you seen him. — Trusting all is [illegible] hope [illegible] are well, I'll close from your loving son [illegible] xx

Adresse

Mrs J. A. Smith
41, Bloxwich Rd,
Walsall,
Staffs
Eng.

PASSION AND TESTAMENT

Clink, clink, clink,
The wind rattles the pole of the fluttering flag.
A wind of change,
Time to stop and re-arrange.
The cross of St George, my England, my church.
To the rear fields of green,
Peace, quiet, and ducks on lakes.

Thirteen bells and time to spare,
Instead of stopping to stare,
Why not visit there.
Cirencester Parish church,
Within is the chapel of St Catherine,
And holding altars to St Christopher,
St Nicholas and St Anthony.

A marvellous stone carved vaulted ceiling
Concealing below the blessed sacrament
Perpetually gilded.
This chapel altar would have a likeness
To the resting place for the Holy Grail.
Upon the altar rests an open book,
You may wish to take a look.

Blues, reds, yellows and greens,
All lit to be seen.
Flowing are the colours of stained glass.
From roof to the marble floor
Are ancient plaster walls
Revealing painted glimpses
Of frescos.

Six tall are the candelabra life light candles
To scare away the fright, into the night.
Inspiration comes forth through large colour windows.
On to the altar of duty shine rays of light,
Highlighting in the North Aisle
Two Gloucestershire Regiment flags,
A silent wind of remembrance.

Yesteryear's music hums and descends
Like circling mist to my ears
After all these years,
My great Uncle Herbert,
A Christian and Violinist,
A proud owner of a rich bass voice.
He was a member of the Gloucestershire Regiment.

When Bristol's Own was founded,
Herbert Fenton Byrne enlisted.
A life commission, his name placed
On the roll of honour.
Aged 24 during the 1916 war
His life did end,
As did his best friends.

No need to wail at the wooden altar rail
After a while in the aisle,
A prayer is all that is needed,
For his church was
St Mary on the Quay in Bristol.
This chapel is a small part
Of the large parish church.

'A' Coy. 12th Battalion, The Gloucestershire Regiment
Bristol's own: Herbert Fenton Byrne - 1915 - Front Right, Seated.

THE SPIRIT OF LYNMOUTH

A charming dramatic seaquest song, all year long.
Lynmouth's intriguing energising Exmoor Valley.
Behold the beauty and danger, nature's strange behaviour.
The mysterious sweeping river to the sea.
Look for treats, high noon Devon cream teas,
With the full ripeness of strawberries.

Hear the graceful essence, the magical call,
The updraught smoke mist of the waterfall.
Airy bouncing water flying through air like shattered glass.
Sprightly sprinkling dances of light rest supreme,
On vivid green, amidst ye old rock foliage hills.
Low tree branches greet passing rippling water smiles.
Passionately the river's life romances onward to the noble sea,
Like Lynmouth lovers, to become one, with each other.

THE MORPHEUS MYTHOLOGY POOL

Avernus,
An underworld of lovelies.
Achaeron, Styx.
Exquisite beauties of the shimmering shadows.
The water's lament, life in the liquid hangs heavy.
Slow incandescent light,
Multicoloured electric green shades.
Sunbeams light the darkness to Hades.
Hidden fences, holding the rocks with trees at bay.
The sundial of time is mine.
A sensual songbird, sent by Orpheus, sings.
Chalice Well opens, deep water echo chambers.
There are no flowers here.
Starbeams of the mystical moon
Reflecting surface tension.
An Aeolus breeze
Tears the elements at the water's shield.
Drinking from Lethe to refresh ourselves,
Revealing cascading colours.
Charon rests easy, it's all in a day.
Elysium is where the heart stays.
Wave goodbye to Iris, on the rainbow path.
There is no room for Narcissus on the mythical carpet,
For this is a place of sleep and dreams.

WOODLANDS REACH

Scampering squirrels,
Choral song birds.
Dancing hours,
Bright sunlit flowers.

Sea air fragrant talk,
Along the tangle wooded walk,
Of heaven's silent scents.
The people's park presents.

The oracle,
Grove Parks,
Grand bandstand,
For thanksgiving days and sporadic parades.

Somerset rhythms of Western light.
Sunset scarlet, and wood green nights.
In the emerald shade of everglade.
The prayer of the park, to the song of the lark.

Refer to Weston's 'Grove Park' 'Garden of Fragrance' on 'The Seashore Trail' Map. Page 62

The Fish Pond, Grove Park, Weston-super-Mare.

ICELAND, THE EMERALD ISLE

Rum drum propellant oars, to Icelandic shores.
Out of the blue, on to the green!
Fearless Berserk warriors sailed North Atlantic saga seas.
Scandinavian Norsemen, Irish Pilgrim Fathers
A crusading genetic clock at Smokey Bay dock.
Ahead of the crowd, 874 AD, Ingolfur Arnarson stood proud.

Emerald exploits, flowing to rhythms of the sea.
Holy Fathers looking for peace and harmony.
Shades of Irish moss upon black lava frost.
Serene sea Ireland trips passing wild Viking long ships.
A Faxa Bay culture cell.
Egil, the Viking warrior poet did tell
Of Eric Bloodaxe, the mighty Viking known so well.
A common ancestry, Icelandic fish and trips you see!

METAL RHYTHMS

Catalytic convertibles call the tune,
Metal rhythm hear my rune,
Oh to become a loon.
Metal Gods in a tin can world,
Silver dream machines,
Looking through grey tinted glass.
Oh what a farce or is it just fast.
Pleasures and leisures,
Out on the range, the symbol,
Jamming, twin-camming, jewel in the crown,
Oh what a clown.
Flash with the cash, dreams of machines;
Nightmare of players, fools of the cabs,
Pawn of the brokers.
Friends of the stokers, cities become real chokers.
High speed to be sustained, but never obtained,
What little gain.
More admissions for more commissions.
How will you pay,
'TODAY?'
Space rocket moon gods at the heart of the machine,
Feelings so vain.
Chariot cadets from a forgotten age,
Just a stoneage rage.
The rising sun sets at dawn,
Tomorrow's new born, to adorn the front lawn,
Oh what a yawn.
Lacerated fuselages of forgotten gods in a rusty world.
Dreams rusting for lust, smooth to choose,
Inflight refuelling, who are they fooling.
Solar wheels, on your heels.

Elemental plates, what is your fate,
Is it too late.
Three,
Two,
One,
Ignition.

FAITH

Oncoming aquamarine holysee, thy perpetual Lordship sails.
Beware a surreal ocean.
Fragile the fire and ice, geothermal springs sing forth.
God knows you in the future, the distance past, always a relative.
When cheering becomes silent as sudden snow mist,
Be not afraid, ask, how much further Father to still clear holy
Mineral waters,
Beyond bubbling hot springs and muddled mudpots,
Where no one seems to care?
Light tones of night sun, more to life than light and shade.
With purple reaching hands, the sea's shine.
Steadfast the weathered lighting anchor, tethered to blade arrows
Of shivering ice.
Shrouded is the frosted silken mask, cloaked as sails in wind.
A trampoline web of intrigue.
Hot flushed steam vents shout, stretching in waves, to the milky
Skies.
Bejewelled spiritual soul cloudscapes flurry together,
Consulting infinity, amongst celestial stars.
Every last drop of fresh evaporated divine thoughts,
Pour from the heavens to dent the darkness of speeding
Fathomless waters, dancing and twisting passing angular glaciers
With uproarious cries.
Spawning lava flows cannot hold captive scorched white light.
From the exploding trees of knowledge come the evangelical
Phoenix songbirds, singing their tune with a sonic boom,
Greeting the arrival in God's acre the voiceless dusk.
White doves take flight over arctic lunar enchanted wonders,
The beauty of invisibility.
Thus far, the secret, to pass through the web.
As footsteps in snow disappear, your trust in
God will appear.

TIME STORM COVE

Tilting of an antique clock, unexpectedly time stops.
Serenity brings forth forgotten thoughts,
Like falling rain from blue sky.
Past times reflecting a straight connection with the future.
Our ancestors, built ornamental walk-ways in the sky
To keep their feet dry.
Breezy sea spray memories com'th forth, the war like
Onslaught of splendid paddle steamers.
Today mere dancing shadows preside at the Old Pier side.
No more melodramatic induced clanks on smooth wooden planks
The grandeur of dusky sepia postcards, capturing a faded
Haze for all to be amazed.
Exhilarated, sat the workers, high and low on boulder ledges,
Pondering amidst impregnable orange sun glints of quirky
Craggy rocks.
Refreshed, rested voyagers posed a tranquil picture.
Yet no time for a smile, relaxation lasts a short while.
Jubilant and serene, the glittering sunlit slipway,
Part submerged, moisten by wallowing sea brine.
Songs of white waters wash, assimilating over worn cliff-stones,
Oblivious to traces of yesterday's diminishing footsteps
At Anchor Head Cove.
All at sea on this present day, the splash, the dash of waves
Carrying ye olde clandestine voices, capture with each rapture
And roar, as though names of half heard conversations with
Spirits of sweeping skies.
Pause not, as the jaded stranger shuffles past, asking.
'Have you got the right time.'
Suffice to say, the right time is now,
It's all around you.

Refer to Anchor Head Cove on 'The Seashore Trail' Map Page 62

Anchor Head

PILGRIMS STANDFAST

Polished flagstones gleam with the aura
Of gleeful cold stone walls,
Warmed by the flickering candle's glow.
Rustling winds from an open door, hit the tiled floor,
Moving pointing fingers of light.
Beckoning the inquisitor to great heights.

Cloistered enlightenment, the three levels,
Different times, the same place.
Reflections of magnificent mosaic's, amidst
Wonders of two sided images, pictures in glass.
Shrouded three dimensional movement,
A time continuum of light.

Colours mirror an artist's palette, sequential segments
Set within a mild misty mist.
Pure thoughts of the altar arena,
Elevated skyward offerings sent past
Stout steadfast timber beams
Hoping for a glance from the heavenly fields of dance.

CHRISTIAN RETURNS THANKS FOR VICTORY

FUTURE VENTURER

Who would steal from the spider's web,
The dewdrops that nature shares.
Snow-capped mountain heartlands,
Frozen edges melted by spring.
Harmonious new life comes forth;
Water cracking the green ice revolution.
Reborn soil, dismissing the toil of the chilled night.

An early morning cultivated.
The cool breeze freshens away the freeze.
Water vaporised,
Clouds shower the multitude of life.
Swollen streams with sharp blades of grass,
Ears to the distance disorderly winds.

Sunlight's umbilical cord, blessed the fertile
Green peculiar peat,
What a feat.
Reap before the fragmentary retreat.
A genesis circle of circumstance,
The science of nature's forces.
A visionary view for more than the few.

GILLS AND FINS

Wizardry wise, yet not despised, flirting with danger.
Fins always not what they appear, the cordon bleu Cassandra
In a swirling deep, dark concealed place.
Stark, mute, motionless, before it, fools gold.
How did it survive to be this old.

Blood and thunder it's staying under, a swish and swipe
Of posture, turbulent, hungry, deliberate assembly.
Focusing wide angled lens, teasing temptation on the barbed hook,
A darting barbed glance, reflection, refraction, reaction.

Everything is moving, seen it all before, a prognostic
Just waiting the tug, rocking and reeling, the line chime sings.
Flashing silver twirling, inviting inquisitors, look who's biting.
Perhaps they will get away with the risk, no harm to try,
Just a fat fly.

The cold side beckons, a missile lightning strike,
Projectile force alined to its purpose.
Waters edge blur, flipping manic panic.
Hook line and sinker, a real stinker,
That old icon was a thinker.

A young fool left to drool, tethered, panting gills,
Gasping for life. An excited cry, is it Cassandra?
Oh, it's just Midas comes the reply, an appreciative
Radiant wry smile, caught every week, never unique.

SON ET LUMIÈRE

England's petite nautical Norman church, St Nicholas.
A high altar apex oasis, green Uphill downs
Sound swept by howling savanna winds.
Wondrous panoramic views, fluttering Chalkhill Blues.
A time out of time, sweet Aromatic Thyme.
Dark Viking hours, treading on Yellow Rock Rose,
From the flame, to the crest;
The returning rambling robin constructs her nest.

Seafaring limestone pavement floor, exulting standing tall.
The spirit of the seas, the swashbuckling Weston breeze.
Nature's propellant pulse, ascending a marine shell sorrow,
Nay, the morrow embraces thick round twig hedges
Spaced in abandonment, like a lonely glacier lake
Awaiting the caressing dance of Easter's green wake.

Refer to Uphill on 'The Seashore Trail' Map Page 62

ANCIENT PARISH CHURCH OF ST NICHOLAS (UPHILL)

HIGH LIFE

There is a place, a sea, above the sea.
Set on a pier, upon a golden sandy beach,
With lots of fun and excitement as you enter,
Its called the Weston-super-Mare Sealife Centre.
You can walk across the deep ocean floor,
Stand with a spine-tingling glare without a care,
A submariners view, eye to eye with a shark
Wow, all the fun of this fabulous aquatic park.

Outside on the beach, make a splash Weston dash,
Into the tide, time and again;
Wave upon wave of exhilaration we crave,
Along the seaside path, games of hide and seek,
A super surf rise, the flowing retreat,
Steady as she goes, the sealords treat.

Refer to Sealife Centre on 'The Seashore Trail' Map Page 62

HEAVEN SCENT

Behold,
Your wonders.
Treasures to embrace,
Your incarnate race.
I look to the sacred scent,
The velvet rose.
I look to the innocent gaze
Of your begotten babes.
I look to the witness glare,
Your empty grave.
Awake in Jesus
See the first light.
Open your heart
To pray each night.

HEART-RENDING

YOU have passed through time
Diana, touched hearts like mine.
Your beauty, always to be young
Your mission just begun.
To those who struggled in need
You reached with heart-warming deeds.
A touch, a smile
Oh so fragile.
Simply to do good
You were often misunderstood
Flashing white lights stripped you bare
Your heart was only to care.
Your dignity assured
The Royal Standard Flag caressed
The People's Princess.
Now you rest with heaven's best.
The People's Princess, Queen of Hearts.

QUEEN OF HEARTS.

LOVELORN

Pray, what is this mystical magical garden paradise,
With its consuming obscuration and tangled undergrowth.
Sudden spring air changes to the petulant dark of night.
Wild weather chills with warbling trills.

Blushful blizzards blow transparent leaves,
Falling to freeze from barren trees.
Lush to slush, the ritual rippling running waters gush.
Sacred stings of panging hail, where is the grail.

Love and hate cogitate in a nameless wilderness.
Frantic feelings are frail.
Night flowers, black and white.
Rouge, lips of rose, coated with waxed dew of dawn.

A strange place at the end of the world, the triangle.
Phosphorescent vision of rain fall on a sunlit day.
We raise our eyes to the big skies,
A place with light and mind rainbows.

Flickering, the lone patrol of a Venus magenta moon,
Enchanting marble dusky atmospheric highs.
Swirling with the breath of God.
Devotion of the broken heart, a shooting star, a servant of dreams.

A rigor chill, the screech of an unseen cat,
The Linnet lost to a hostile restless wind.
Who knows this garden of trickery.
People looking to find their dreams.

This maelstrom paradise,
A dangerous place to be,
With silhouette smiles leading to the aisles.
When the weather turns, hearts rhythmically churn.

FORETHOUGHT

I am
Not the same person I used to be.
At least that is how it seems to me.
I walk a little slower now
Like footsteps on water will I submerge and sink.
You see I think,
I am not the person I used to be
At least that is how it feels to me.

Every ocean floor leads to the shore
Wisdom is a lifelong friend
Remember your loved for who you are
Open your eyes and you will see
The people you know
Are not the same as they used to be.

LONG DISTANCE 1-9-1-2.

Double ring, double ring,
A bell like the crow's nest ring,
Pulsates along the brown cord
Of the black bakelite phone
In my home.

It is nineteen ninety eight
As I contemplate
The call.
'Hello Anthony, it is Millvina.'
My mind davits as if to descend.

Propelled, down to The Grand Oak Staircase,
An unmistakable fact
Is to consider that,
My friend is the youngest survivor
From the 'Titanic' ocean liner.

Anthony Keyes with Millvina Dean the youngest 'Titanic' survivor
February 20th 1998

THE SEASHORE TRAIL

WESTON-SUPER-MARE SEASHORE TRAIL

The Severn Estuary is a site of international significance and the Weston-super-Mare Seashore Trail is a sensitive poetic experience and celebration of the coast.

Travelling along the poetry trail which covers approximately 6 miles you can visit splendid viewing points along the Somerset coastal areas of Weston-super-Mare, from Uphill to Middle Hope Cove and including Weston's 'Grove Park Garden of Fragrance.'

This new and exciting Seashore Trail has access 7 days a week. The Trail can be joined at any of the eight locations and followed on foot, bike or accessed by car.

Anthony Keyes' Seashore Trail promotes both the built and cultural heritage of the Somerset coast bringing together the disciplines of environment, geology, history, landscape and tourism in a wider dimension.

The coast is a resource for pleasure and leisure the poems encourage you to become actively involved in the trail.

Anthony Keyes, has poetry published in 41 different books. His original idea for a Weston-super-Mare Seashore Poetry Trail uses eight of his Weston poems.

These poems are all featured in this book.

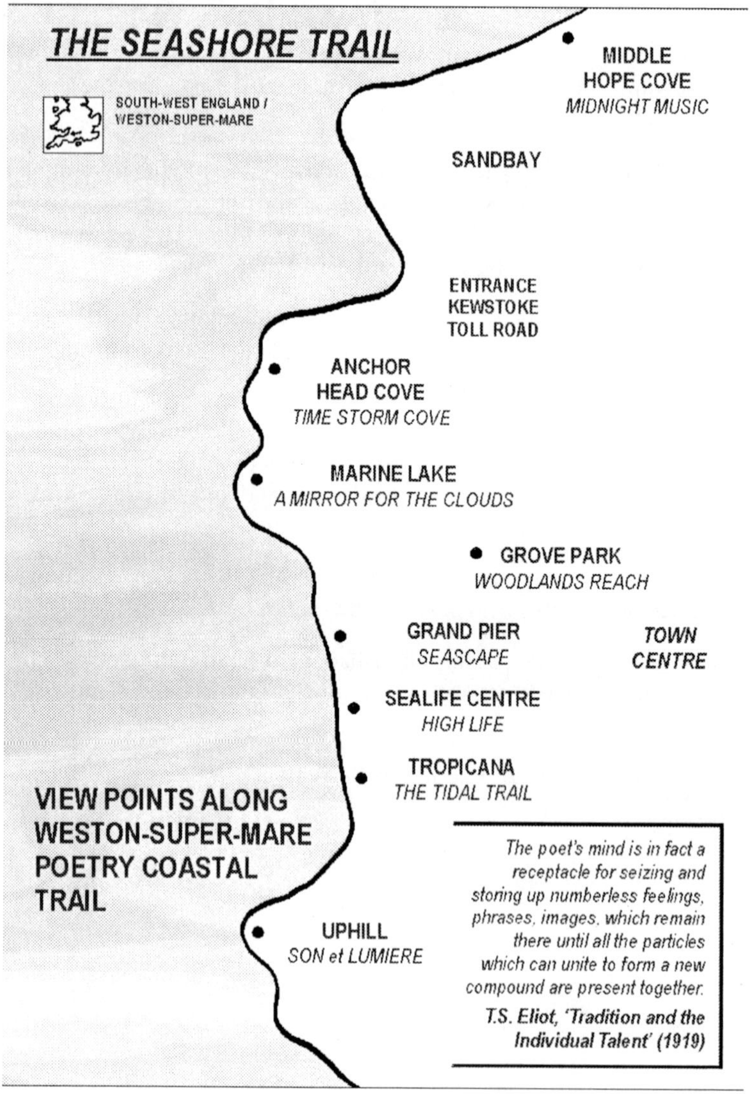
THE SEASHORE TRAIL
SOUTH-WEST ENGLAND / WESTON-SUPER-MARE
MIDDLE HOPE COVE
MIDNIGHT MUSIC
SANDBAY
ENTRANCE KEWSTOKE TOLL ROAD
ANCHOR HEAD COVE
TIME STORM COVE
MARINE LAKE
A MIRROR FOR THE CLOUDS
GROVE PARK
WOODLANDS REACH
GRAND PIER
SEASCAPE
TOWN CENTRE
SEALIFE CENTRE
HIGH LIFE
TROPICANA
THE TIDAL TRAIL
VIEW POINTS ALONG WESTON-SUPER-MARE POETRY COASTAL TRAIL
UPHILL
SON et LUMIERE
The poet's mind is in fact a receptacle for seizing and storing up numberless feelings, phrases, images, which remain there until all the particles which can unite to form a new compound are present together.
T.S. Eliot, 'Tradition and the Individual Talent' (1919)

THE SEASHORE TRAIL

Poem Extracts

'Wave compositions serenade Middle Hope Cove
As the full blooded sun drowns to silence.
A lullaby sunset flashes colours to their sleep.'

(Midnight Music) See page 8

'Breezy sea spray memories com'th forth, the war like
Onslaught of splendid paddle steamers.'

(Time Storm Cove) See page 44

'At Glentworth Bay
A Marine Lake
Weston's mirror for the clouds.'

(A Mirror For The Clouds)
See page 26

'Somerset rhythms of Western light.
sunset scarlet, and wood green nights.'

(Woodlands Reach) See page 38

'We laugh, and cry.
For we came to rest our hearts
Beneath a Weston sky.'

(Seascape) See page 12

'You can walk across the deep oceans floor,
Stand with a spine-tingling glare without a care,
A submariners view, eye to eye with a shark.'

(High Life) See page 52

'I thought I saw your golden light
In the breaking waves of the Tropicana night.'

(The Tidal Trail) See page 6

'Seafaring limestone pavement floor, exulting, standing tall
The spirit of the seas, the swashbuckling Weston breeze.'

(Son et Lumière) See page 50

For those who wish to know more about Weston-super-Mare, Anthony Keyes is the author of the best selling book titled Weston-super-Mare The Sands of Time which is an illustrated history of one of England's most famous seaside towns.

The book traces the town's development from the Victorian era to the present day and is packed with period photographs and illustrations, together with a Comprehensive accompanying commentary.

A perfect high quality souvenir, first published in 1995 by Sigma Leisure, reprinted in 1998, cover price £6.95. A treasure trove of memories for residents and tourists alike.

ISBN: 1 85058 470 2

REFERENCE AND COMMENTS:

* **Guardian Angel**
Published: What a Wonderful World - Triumph House, 1996.
Comments: North Somerset Poetry Contest Highly Commended.

* **Wisdom For Change**
Published: Poets in the West Country - Arrival Press, 1996.
Comments: North Somerset Poetry Contest Commended.

Charlotte
Published: Missing You - Arrival Press, 1997.

The Tidal Trail
Published: West Country Rhythms - Arrival Press, 1997.
Comments: Weston-super-Mare - Seashore Trail.

Midnight Music
Published: Rhythm 'n' Rhyme - Arrival Press, 1996.
Comments: Weston-super-Mare - Seashore Trail.

* **Storm Tears**
Published: Bridging the Gap - Anchor Books, 1994.
Comments: South Woodspring Poetry Contest -Highly Commended.
(With Additional Line)
Published: Friends Forever - Arrival Press, 1994.
Comments: Arrival Press - Publishers Medal Award.

* **The Festival**
Published: Poetry Now Regional Anthology, West Country 1995.
Comments: South Woodspring Poetry Contest- Highly Commended.

* **Reconciliation**
Published: Royal Poets - Arrival Press, 1995
Comments: North Somerset Poetry Contest - Highly Commended.
To commemorate the 50th anniversary of the ending of World War Two.

Seascape
Published: Sun, Sea and Chips - Arrival Press, 1996.
Comments: Weston-super-Mare - Seashore Trail.

* **Orchestra of Light**
Published: Feels Like Heaven - Triumph House, 1996.
Comments:North Somerset Poetry Contest - Very Highly Commended.

* **Haworth Hearts**
(Inspired by the Lives of the Brontë Sisters)
Published: Heart of the Matter - Arrival Press, 1995.
Comments: North Somerset Poetry Contest - Highly Commended.

* **Crystal Clear**
Published: The Arrival Press Poetry Companion, 1995.
Comments: North Somerset Poetry Contest - Highly Commended.

Legacy
Published: Pulse Rate Rising - Arrival Press, 1995.
Comments: 'A Lovely Poem, Much Appreciated' Stanley Matthews.

* **Star Light**
Published: Triumph House Collection 1996.
Comments: North Somerset Poetry Contest - Highly Commended.

* **Park Street 1920**
Published: Emergency - Poetry Now, 1996.
Comments: North Somerset Poetry Contest - Highly Commended.

* **Sonnet 59-15**
Published: Blaze of Glory - Poetry Now, 1996.
Comments: North Somerset Poetry Contest - Highly Commended.

A Mirror for the Clouds
Published: Just Visiting - Arrival Press, 1997.
Comments: Weston-super-Mare - Seashore Trail.

*** Liquid Dreams**
Published: Messages from the Muse - Poetry Now, 1994.
Comments: South Woodspring Poetry Contest -
Highly Commended.

Glacier Garden
Published: Spring is in the Air - Arrival Press, 1996.

A Shout in the Dark
Published: Distant Memories - Arrival Press, April 1997.
Comments: Performed by Anthony Keyes 15th April 1997
And Broadcast by BBC Radio Commemorating the 85th
Anniversary of the sinking of the ill-fated Liner - 'Titanic' - The
World's largest ship.
'The poem gives a sense of the hopelessness of the situation
as the liner was overwhelmed'
Southampton City Heritage.

800 Limited Edition 'Titanic' Postcards.
Poem published in The Evening Post 16th January 1998 - Postcard with poem published in Weston & Worle News 15th January 1998 - Weston & Somerset Mercury 23rd January 1998.
Published to coincide with the release of James Cameron's Blockbuster Film 'Titanic' - 23rd January 1998 and Anthony Keyes 16 week long 'Titanic' exhibition at Weston-super-Mare.

Passion & Testament
Published: Poets Retreat - Anchor Books, 1996.
Comments: BBC Radio Bristol & Somerset Sound Feature - September 1996.
To commemorate the 80th Anniversary of the Bloody First World War Somme Battlefields.

The Spirit of Lynmouth
Published: Natural Beauty - Poetry Now, 1996.

*** Morpheus Mythology Pool**
Published: Simple Pleasures - Poetry Now, 1994.
Comments: South Woodspring Poetry Contest -
Highly Commended.

Woodlands Reach
Published: Words of Worship - Triumph House, 1996.
Comments: Weston-super-Mare. Seashore Trail. 'Garden of Fragrance' (Grove Park)

Iceland, The Emerald Isle
Published: Hot Off The Press - Poetry Now, 1996.

* **Metal Rhythms**
Published: Poetry Now 1994 West Country Anthology.
Comments: South Woodspring Poetry Contest -
Highly Commended.

Faith
Published: Christian Verse from Western England - Triumph House, 1996.

Time Storm Cove
Published: At The Third Stroke - Poetry Now, 1996.
Comments: Weston-super-Mare, Seashore Trail.

* **Pilgrims Standfast**
Published: Poem's Of the 90's - Poetry Now, 1995.
Comments: North Somerset Poetry Contest - Highly Commended.

* **Future Venturer**
Published: Life on the Land - Arrival Press, 1995.
Comments: South Woodspring Poetry Contest -
Highly Commended.

* **Gills & Fins**
Published: Poets Angle - Poetry Now, 1995.
Island Moods & Reflections, 1995 -
Poetry Institute of the British Isles.
Comments: Judged in top 10% received in Contest of
Great Britain, 1995.
South Woodspring Poetry Contest - Highly Commended.

Son et Lumière
Published: Voices of the Heart - The Poetry Guild of Great Britain, 1997 Comments: 'The poem exhibits true literacy excellence' - The Poetry Guild.
Tranquil Thoughts - Triumph House, 1997
Weston-super-Mare Seashore Trail.

High Life
Published: Fair Ground Attractions - Arrival Press, 1996.
Comments: Weston-super-Mare, Seashore Trail.

Heaven Scent
Published: Golden Praise - Triumph House, 1997.

Heart-Rending
Published: Poems for a Princess - In Memory of Diana,
Princess of Wales, 1961-1997 - Anchor Books, 1998.
Diana - a Tribute to the People's Queen of Hearts.
1961-1997 - Arrival Press, 1998.
Western Daily Press - Saturday September 6th, 1997.
A tribute to Diana, Princess of Wales - in memory, on the day of her funeral - Saturday 6th September 1997.
Comments: Broadcast on Radio 5 Live, John Inverdale- Nationwide, 4th September 1997.
'A moving tribute' poem. Diana, Princess of Wales, Memorial Committee.

* **Lovelorn**
Published: All for Love - Anchor Books, 1995.
Comments: North Somerset Poetry Contest - Highly Commended.

Forethought
Published: Moments in Life - Anchor Books, 1997.

Long Distance 1-9-1-2. Previously unpublished.

* These poems were entered for competition.